T0113538

Why Not With JESUS?

Pastor Bim Folayan

WESTBOW
PRESS®
A DIVISION OF THOMAS NELSON
& ZONDERVAN

Keys for other Bible translations used in this book:
AMP – The Amplified Bible
GNT – Good News Translation
MSG – The Message Bible
NCV – New Century Version
NIV – New International Version
NKJV – New King James Version
NLT – New Living Translation
TLB – Living Bible

WestBow Press books may be ordered through
booksellers or by contacting:

WestBow Press
A Division of Thomas Nelson & Zondervan
1663 Liberty Drive
Bloomington, IN 47403
www.westbowpress.com
1 (866) 928-1240

ISBN: 978-1-9736-0044-2 (sc)
ISBN: 978-1-9736-0045-9 (e)

Print information available on the last page.

WestBow Press rev. date: 10/5/2017

Contents

DEDICATION

Dedicated to CET-c Rochester
and Essex 2015 team

"But to us there is but one God, the Father, of whom are all things, and we in him; and one Lord Jesus Christ, by whom are all things, and we by him"
-1 Corinthians 8:6

It is true that through the sin of one-man death began to rule because of that one man. But how much greater is the result of what was done by the one man, Jesus Christ! All who receive God's abundant grace and are freely put right with him will rule in life through Christ. **18**So then, as the one sin condemned all people, in the same way the one righteous act scts all people free and gives them life.
-Romans 5:17 18 (GNT)

Neither is thcre salvation in any other: for there is none other name under heaven given among men, whereby we must be saved.
- Acts 4:12

'He fed them
He led them
And bled for them.

Serving them
Saving them,
And Sending them.'

Bim Folayan
July 2015

Introduction

God was in Christ, making peace
between the world and himself. In Christ,
God did not hold the world guilty of its sins.
And he gave us this message of peace.
(2 Corinthians 5:19 NCV)

For God so loved the world that He qualifies us as sons. We didn't have to qualify, but He justified us (John 3:16, 1 John 3:1). His mercy reaches out to man giving him the real life, hope and peace.

The Truth of His written Word assures us full redemption. God, through grace, gave His only begotten Son to a dying world to die instead, that we may live and have life to the full (John 3:17, John 10:10). His name is Jesus and through Him came the fullness of God to man. Colossians 2:9 *"For in him dwelleth all the fulness of the Godhead bodily."* Whoever has the Son has The Life (of God), for this life is in the Son. Acts 4:12 *"Neither is there salvation in any other: for there is none other name under heaven given among men, whereby we must be saved."*

Until a man submits to the Lordship of Jesus, he does not know God, for Jesus is **the Way** (to God and His ways), **the Truth** (actuality) and **Life** (the real life). No one can know the Father but BY JESUS (John 14:6). Life without God (in Christ) is empty and lived in vain.

Salvation of man through Christ is God's greatest gift to mankind (John 3:16) and everyone must avail themselves of this **goodness**!

"O taste and see that the Lord is good:
blessed is the man that trusteth in him"
(Psalm 34:8)

Chapter One

Sent to Save Us

"But because of his great love for us, God, who is rich in mercy, ^{5} made us alive with Christ even when we were dead in transgressions— it is by grace you have been saved" (Ephesians 2:4-5 NIV).

God sent Jesus Christ His only begotten Son that we may live. *"And this is life eternal, that they might know thee the only true God, and Jesus Christ, whom thou hast sent."* (John 17:3). God made man in His image to conform to His image and manner, but man deviated from his Maker, God therefore, abundant in grace and mercy, restored man to Himself through Christ because *"**Salvation is found in no one else**, for there is no other name under heaven given to mankind by which we must be saved"* (Acts 4:12 NIV). Salvation is a package. It comprises of blessings and advantages ranging from redemption to living a successful, victorious, triumphant, abundant and eternal life (2 Peter 1:3). Being in Christ gives us the unique advantage that puts us ahead in life and the Bible says we shall reign with Him. *"much more they which receive abundance of grace and of the gift of righteousness shall reign in life by one, Jesus Christ* (Romans 5:17).

We see in John 1:16 and in the above passage that by the fullness of Christ in us, we are granted the abundance of grace and the gift of righteousness. What a huge gift to also be made right with God. Wonderful! We therefore do not have to work for it but only to receive these gifts by faith. There is no qualification required! Glory and thanks be to God! Romans 8:1 attest that there is now no condemnation (whatsoever) to those who are Christ Jesus. *"If the Son therefore shall make you free, ye shall be free indeed"* (John 8:36).

Romans 3:23 state that all have sinned and fallen short of God's glory. In His mercy, He offered Jesus Christ His Son as propitiation for our sins. Christ in His generosity offered Himself as sacrifice for the world, suffering a precarious death on the cross for our sins. *"He personally carried the load of our sins in his own body when he died on the cross so that we can be finished with sin and live a good life from now on. For his wounds have healed ours!"* (1 Peter 2:24 TLB). 1 John 2:2 refers to Him as the atoning sacrifice for our sins.

By this act of selflessness, we are completely free from guilt and shame, made righteous and no longer offenders. We have now been given new and beautiful life, having been purified. We have been given victorious life and power over sin (Romans 6:14). This salvation package gives us dominion and victory. 1 John 5:4 says *"For whatsoever is born of God overcometh the world: and this is the victory that overcometh the world, even our faith."* Faith in Christ Jesus delivers peace and the light of God on our path. This is made possible by the wound and pain He suffered in our stead (Isaiah 53:5) to redeem us from darkness to light and from death to life.

By this generosity, Christ's painful death for our redemption has brought us into being partakers of His divine nature. By this, we become an associate of His kind of life. This new life (Zoë) is God's kind of life. It is imperishable and enduring (1 Peter 1:23). Christ's suffering and sacrifice has purchased this for us. 1 Peter 1:11 speaks of the suffering of Christ and the glory that must follow. We have become His glory, born for glorious living. Christ has paid the price.

This package of Christ's salvation delivers unto us a brand new and eternal life (John 3:16). By this, the old life is gone and the new life takes over. *"Therefore, if any man be in Christ, he is a new creature: old things are passed away; behold, all things are become new."* (2 Corinthians 5:17). The Bible says Jesus is the only way whereby men must be saved (Acts 4:12). It therefore means that there is salvation in no other than Christ. Neither can there be any other foundation except one laid by Christ (1 Corinthians 3:11).

"...the Father sent the Son to be the Saviour of the world" (1 John 4:14). He is the only true and firm foundation that offers the means whereby men can be saved (1 John 5:20). He is the Light and darkness cannot over-power

the light in Him. He was in the beginning with God and one with God. He is the Word and the Word is God (John 1:1). Jesus is Lord! He is one with God, the express image of the Father. The Bible (God's Word) tells us that Jesus is Lord. He is true image of God.

He was revealed in Isaiah - *"I, even I, am the Lord; and beside me there is no saviour"* (Isaiah 43:11). God is love, for out of love, He offered His son to save us (John 3:16). He is love personified through Jesus who died in our place so that our offences are pardoned and our sins blotted away. By surrendering our lives over to Him in full submission, life becomes purposeful and meaningful. Life saved and brought into newness. The life He supplants in us is the real life. As many that has been brought into this new life become God's people (a new race in Christ -1 Peter 2:9), special species, created unto good works (Ephesians 2:10).

True life is life lived in Christ Jesus; For in Him, all things consist (Colossians 1:17). Life without Christ goes nowhere, because except a man be Born-Again, the Bible says He cannot see the kingdom of God. This

Kingdom is only for those saved through Christ. God gave Jesus Christ that whoever believes in Him will not perish but have life eternal (with Him in this Kingdom).

Man perishes when He is not anchored to His Maker, he suffers when he is not connected to his Source but life is meaningful and with direction (John 6:33) when Jesus is Lord over his live. When Jesus reigns in our lives, we live the significant life. *"For His divine power has bestowed on us [absolutely] everything necessary for [a dynamic spiritual] life and godliness, through true and personal knowledge of Him who called us by His own glory and excellence."* (2 Peter 1:3 Amp). It is only through Christ's salvation that we come to God's glory and perfection (Acts 4:12). Jesus is a Friend that sticks closer than a brother (Proverbs 18:24). We can depend on Him because He is ever faithful and ever sure. Jesus is always there and will always be there when no one is there for you (Hebrews 13:5). He will not fail nor forsake you for He does not disappoint. He will not give-up on you nor be tired of you. In His Word, He says that He will abide with us always -everywhere and forever in the Person of the Holy Spirit (who is just like Him), whom He refers to as another Comforter/Advocate (John 14:16) but this only happens when our hearts are in whole-hearted devotion to Him. He is our Stand-by. Hebrews 7:25 NKJV states, *"Therefore He is also able to save to the uttermost those who come to God through Him, since He always lives to make intercession for them."* He will abide with you and He will support you. God is ever faithful; His abiding presence is always available to those know Him (Luke 11:13).

How do you begin to know Jesus intimately? You start by giving Him genuine and whole-hearted invitation for His Lordship over your life in full submission and commitment. Jesus, one with God, the Father, He is the Son and He is the Holy Spirit. He is 3 in 1 and 1 in 3. He is Lord and the express image of the Father. *"The Son is the radiance of God's glory and* **the exact representation of his being**, *sustaining all things by his powerful word. After he had provided purification for sins, he sat down at the right hand of the Majesty in heaven."* – (Hebrews 1:3 NIV).

God pardons the repentant heart. A repentant action gives God pleasure; a demonstration of the Father's love and mercy as depicted with the parable of the lost son (Luke 15:11-32). God wipes out our sins, keeping no record because He is faithful and just to forgive as the Bible records us in 1 John 1:9. The Book of Joel 2:32 states that whoever calls on the Name of the Lord shall be saved. Call on Him today, and you will be saved. Ask Him to take over and be responsible for your life. Give Him full submission, do not regress in making today your day of salvation for a fulfilling life. Your transformation is what now matters to God, He will not consider your past mistakes neither will He judge you. He sent Jesus to die for you anyway. He will do anything. Thank God, Jesus did not remain in the grave; He rose for your justification! (Romans 4:25).

God is love (1 John 4:8), full of compassion. His deep affection offers us mercy and grace. In Him is fulfilment and life eternal. Life beyond physical but spiritual. Life hinged on God is filled with purpose and meaning. The Bible spells this out in 1 John 4:9-10 that *"In this was manifested the love of God* *toward us, because that God sent his only begotten Son into the world, **that we might live through him.**[10] **Herein is love**, not that we loved God, but that he loved us, and sent his Son to be the propitiation for our sins."* Sin came into the world through the first man Adam who committed high treason but the second Adam came in the Person of Jesus Christ came to give us new and higher life, redeeming us from the old and sinful Adamic nature we were born with (1 Corinthians 15:45). Why not with Jesus? Only through Him is God's nature given. He is our righteousness, holiness, redemption as well as sanctification (1 Corinthians 1:30). Proverbs 21:21(NKJV) states *"He who follows righteousness and mercy finds life, righteousness, and honour"*. Jesus offers the mercy and honour you deserve. He is the light, the Truth and the way; He is Link to your search. Bible tells us that no one comes to the Father except by Him. It implies that life is meaningless without Him. Life without its Maker is empty. Psalm 24:1(NIV) reminds us that *"The earth is the Lord's, and **everything in it**, the world, and **all who live in it**"*. Through Christ, man is no longer estranged but reinstated to his Maker.

Surrendering to Jesus with a heart of sincerity opens the door to higher life. Life submitted to God to do of His pleasure (Philippians 2:13) finds fulfilment and security. This is done by open invitation according to Romans 10:9 *"That if thou shalt confess with thy mouth the Lord Jesus, and shalt **believe** in thine heart that God hath raised him from the dead, **thou shalt be saved**."* This scripture implies that you make declaration with our mouth that Jesus is Lord of your life and you will be saved/brought over as God's. Man need his Maker to live and reign according to His Maker's design. Man lost it through Adam, but God restored him through Jesus. You too can cross over and be saved today!

The sacrifice that offers man new life came through Christ, the Son of God. In Him is redemptive power. Accepting Him as Lord and saviour translate from darkness into light, from death (spiritual) to life and from bondage into liberty. *"Who hath delivered us from the power of darkness, and hath translated us into the kingdom of his dear"* (Colossians 1:13).

"Unjustly condemned,
he was led away.
No one cared that he died without
descendants,
that his life was cut short in midstream.
But he was struck down
for the rebellion of my people.
⁹ He had done no wrong
and had never deceived anyone.
But he was buried like a criminal;
he was put in a rich man's grave.
¹⁰ But it was the Lord's good plan to crush
him and cause him grief..."
(Isaiah 53:8-10 NLT)

The love of God for a dying world caused Him to give His Best (John 3:16). God got His Son to pay the ultimate price for the remission of our sins that bought us redemption to Him. Believers in Christ become His children (1 John 3:1), holy and 'unblameable'. No longer subject to sin. *"You have died with Christ and are set free from the ruling spirits of the universe...* (Colossians 2:20 GNT).

Why not with Jesus? He is the Lamb of God that takes away the sin of the world (John 1:29). He justified us and took our guilt and shame away. Only Him was capable to take man from sin to salvation, from destruction to life incorruptible (1 Peter 1:23), from slavery to sonship and from bondage into liberty (Galatians 3:25). By faith in Christ, we take up His nature, Christ's righteousness becomes ours. We become acceptable to God. Romans 8:10 (Amp) accentuate this: *"If Christ lives in you, though your [natural] body is dead because of sin, your spirit is alive because of righteousness [which He provides]."* By Jesus, we come alive to God!

Galatians 3:26-27 states: *"For ye are all the children of God by faith in Christ Jesus. 27 For as many of you as have been baptized into Christ have put on Christ."* The ordinary life is supplanted and divinity takes over. The extra-ordinary life make you relate with God as father. They start to walk in the light as He is in the light. They establish their walk in Him as we have in Acts 17:28 that *"For in Him, we live, and move and have our being...."* They are the offspring (children) of God, created in Christ Jesus (Galatians 3:26-27). This higher life is infused in all who have declared Jesus as Lord over their lives, who then have put on 'the new self', created in the image of God in true holiness and righteousness (Ephesians 4:24). By faith they have believed and are translated into this glorious life.

In Mark 16:16, Jesus said that whoever believes and is baptized shall be saved. Saved from this world system that is bound to fail, saved from destruction, from poverty and from shame and brought into life indestructible. *"He has saved us and called us to a holy life— not because of anything we have done but because of his own purpose and grace. This grace was given us in Christ Jesus before the beginning of time, 10 but it has now been revealed through the appearing of our Savior, Christ Jesus, who has destroyed death and has brought life and immortality to light through the gospel"* (2 Timothy 1:9-10 NIV). What an awesome privilege to be in Christ! Yielding to the saving power of Christ gives us supremacy over Satan, the enemy of our soul. In Christ, we have the authority over his works (Luke 10:19). Life is no longer lived from the stand-point of defeat but victory because of union with Christ. *"But he that is joined unto the Lord is one spirit"* (1 Corinthians 6:17). By this union, we no longer live by whatever life hands down to us but reinstated as victors and not victims. The Bible refers to the new creation as royal and peculiar (1 Peter 2:9).

The new man reigns with Christ. He is programmed for accomplishment if he keeps in faith and in conformity with God's way. This way, He is not vulnerable. He keeps his focus serving God. Through fellowship, he is no longer oblivious. The peace of God in Christ Jesus envelopes him. Jesus said in Matthew 11:28 (NIV), *"Come to me, all you who are weary and burdened, and I will give you rest."* Rest from the cares of the world and its system that is destined to fail. The Bible lets us know that by flesh (carnality) shall no man prevail. This means that it is only through God that we prevail in life. Those who have embraced Christ live in this special rest (Hebrews 4:3). Due to their new birth, they are awakened to the Fatherhood of God, becoming joint-heirs with Christ! (Romans 8:16-17), they reign with Him. They are constantly exhibiting His nature and life - product of re-generated life.

"Then spake Jesus again unto them, saying, I am the light of the world: he that followeth me shall not walk in darkness, but shall have the light of life" (John 8:12). Due to your new nature in Jesus, you become light to your world as He is Light. Light attract, so your light must attract others because your new nature that portrays Christ. Zacchaeus was drawn to Jesus. He was wise to seek Him desperately for change to come to him and his household. He made quick good use of his opportunity and reached for Jesus' attention and he got it despite dissuasions and his physical limitation (Luke 19:1-10). You too can reach for Jesus today. Jesus promised to be in Zacchaeus' house and He was, He will come into your hearts as you invite Him today. Zacchaeus was a rich man but didn't allow pride to prevent him for an opportunity of a life time and beyond. With determination, he sought Jesus for the free-gift of salvation. Like Zacchaeus, simply forsake old ways and embrace intimacy with Jesus. Turn to righteousness and the glorious life available only in Christ Jesus. *"For the Son of man is come to seek and to save that which was lost"* (Luke 19:10).

"Neither is there salvation in any other: for <u>there is none other name under heaven given among men, whereby we must be saved</u>." (Acts 4:12). Receive Him today, so that redemption and restoration to God can be yours! Tomorrow may be too late! You too can walk into extra-ordinary and the supernatural life available in Christ Jesus. You can become His beloved today. Apostle Peter attesting with the early Christians said in 1 Peter 2:3 that they have tasted that **the Lord is good**. So, WHY NOT WITH JESUS?

Begins this vital step now by saying this simple prayer and mean with all your heart:

Dear heavenly Father, I thank you for the precious sacrifice of Your Son, Jesus Christ who died for me that I may be reconciled to You. I thank You for the saving me through His precious blood shed for me. According to Your Word in Romans 10:9-10, I declare with my mouth that Jesus is Lord of my life and I believe with all my heart that you raised Him from the dead for my justification. I repent of all my sins and receive Your forgiveness. I receive the new life today, I am BORN AGAIN. Thank You Lord for saving me.

If you just said that and you mean it, I say Congratulations and welcome to the family of God! All things are new! (2 Corinthians 5:17) *"So now we can **rejoice** in our wonderful new relationship with God because our Lord Jesus Christ has made us friends of God"* (Romans 5:11 NLT). The Book of 1 John 3:1(NIV) states, *"See what great love the Father has lavished on us, that we should be called **children of God**! And that is what we are!"*

You have been saved through the life of God's Son, Jesus Christ (Romans 5:10 NLT). You are God's own purchased and special to God. You now have the gift of righteousness and you will reign with Christ! (Romans 5:17). You have been given fullness of life. Your sins have been forgiven.

"I, even I, am he who blots out
your transgressions, for my own sake,
and remembers your sins no more.
Says God's Word to you in
Isaiah 43:25(NIV).

Therefore, ensure you are not lured back into your past but maintain your stand for Jesus by keeping a focus so you do not retrogress. This was Apostle Peter's admonition:

"Like newborn babies, crave pure spiritual milk, so that by it you may grow up in your salvation, ³ now that you have tasted that the Lord is good" (1 Peter 2:2-3 NIV).

Be strong in this new life in Christ and resist the past temptations (James 4:7). Seek the Truth. God's Word is Truth. Be an obedient and determined student of God's Word (The Bible). The Word of God is God (John 1:1). God and His Word are not separate. Follow God's Word (2 Timothy 3:16-17) learn it and be skilled in His ways and reflect your new nature. Colossians 3:10 (TLB) *"You are living a brand new kind of life that is continually learning more and more of what is right, and trying constantly to be more and more like Christ who created this new life within you."*

Chapter Two

Walking in His Way

*"...But how much greater is the result of what was done by the one man, Jesus Christ! All **who receive** God's abundant grace and are **freely put right with him** will rule in life through Christ".*
(Romans 5:17 GNT)

Welcome to new life in Christ! **Christ in you** the hope of glory (Colossians1:27). The Bible states, *"Therefore if any man be in Christ, he is a new creature: old things are passed away; behold, all things are become new."* (2 Corinthians 5:17). You have become a member of His body, of His flesh, and of his bones (Ephesians 5:30). This portrays how bonded you are with and in Christ. Your life is no longer ordinary for, *"His divine power has given us everything we need for a godly life through our knowledge of him who called us by his own glory and goodness"*

2 Peter 1:3 NIV) and according to Colossians 3:10 (NIV)*"...have put on the new self, which is being renewed in knowledge in the image of its Creator."*

What an awesome privilege!

"...I will call them 'my people' who are not my people; and I will call her 'my loved one' who is not my loved one,"
26 and, "In the very place where it was said to them, 'You are not my people,' there they will be called 'children of the living God"' (Romans 9:25-26 NIV)

Hallelujah! What a redeeming Father!

The Message Bible in Colossians 3:1-2 enjoins thus: *"So if you're serious about living this new resurrection life with Christ,* **act like it. Pursue the things over which Christ presides. Don't shuffle along**, *eyes to the ground, absorbed with the things right in front of you. Look up, and be alert to what is going on around Christ—that's where the action is.* **See things from his perspective.**" It is imperative that now that you belong to God's family, that your life reflect God's traits and

character since you have taken-up His typ
of life and nature (Colossians 3:10 *"And have
put on the new man, which is renewed in
knowledge after the image of him that created
him"*), baptised into Christ (Galatians 3:26-
27) and your spirit recreated after Him with
eternal life implanted into your spirit.

Ephesians 1:3 tell us that being sons, God
has blessed us with every spiritual blessing
in Christ. This then implies taking up His
nature since we are born of Him. According
to John 1:12-13 (NIV) *"...to all who did
receive him, to those who believed in his
name, he gave the right to become children of
God—* [13] *children born not of natural descent,
nor of human decision or a husband's will, but
born of God"*. You have been endowed with
power/ability to function as God's child. Your
spirit has been enabled. In 1 Corinthians
2:12, we read *"Now we have received, not the
spirit of the world, but the spirit which is of
God; that we might know the things that are
freely given to us of God."*

Referring to those who have taken up this
new nature, Apostle Paul said, *"So from now
on we regard no one from a human point of*

iew [according to worldly standards and values]... (2 Corinthians 5:16 (Amp). Being God's children, they are therefore referred to as gods (Psalm 82:6, John 10:34), they become His heirs and representatives (Romans 8:17, 2 Corinthians 5:20). Divine nature is in them because they are born of His flesh and of His bones (Ephesians 5:30). They possess the extra-ordinary and abundant life (1 John 4:4, 2 Peter 1:3-4) coupled with interminable life (John 3:16). They are special breed, peculiar in nature (1 Peter 2:9). They have received power (John 1:12) to relate with their Father in spirit and in truth (John 4:24). They are given special gifts (of the spirit) to function specially for the perfecting of the saints (Christians/Christ-like), for the work of the ministry and for the edifying of the body of Christ/the people of God (Ephesians 4:12).

The extra-ordinary life you now possess is due to your new nature. *"And this is the testimony: God has given us eternal life, and this life is in his Son. 12 Whoever has the Son has life; whoever does not have the Son of God does not have life"* (1 John 5:11-12 NIV). Happy are you if you have the Son. Jesus loves you. Be dedicated to Him without compromise. *"God is a Spirit: and they that worship him must worship him in spirit and in truth"* (John 4:24). Live conscious of who you now are -God's true representative. *"We are therefore Christ's ambassadors..."* (2 Corinthians 5:20). Being engrafted into God's family, you enjoy divine benefits and privileges. Jesus said, *"At that time you won't need to ask me for anything, for <u>you can go directly to the Father</u> and ask him, and he will give you what you ask for because you use my name. ²⁴ You haven't tried this before, **but begin now**. Ask, using my name, and <u>you will receive, and your cup of joy will overflow</u>"* (John 16:23-24 TLB).

Being in Christ, He takes responsibility of your life if He stopped at nothing to save you (Hebrews 12:2). Ensure you are focused, living the life of faith; For without faith it is impossible to please Him (Hebrews 11:6). Set your mind on Christ. Live an authentic Christian life. Avoid compromise. Colossians 3:1-4 (NIV) states *"Since, then, you have been raised with Christ, set your hearts on things above, where Christ is, seated at the right hand of God. ² Set your minds on things above, not on earthly things. ³ For you died, and your life is now hidden with Christ in God.* **⁴** *When Christ, who is your life, appears, then you also will appear with him in glory.* Yes, you died to your old self. So, leave the past behind you and embrace a blessed future (Psalm 1:1-3 NIV).

"Blessed is the one
who does not walk in step with the wicked
or stand in the way that sinners take
or sit in the company of mockers,
² *but whose delight is in the law of the Lord,*
and who meditates on his law, day and night.
³ *That person is like a tree planted by*
streams of water,
which yields its fruit in season
and whose leaf does not wither—
whatever they do prospers".

God's glory reside with those whose lives are consistent with His in deed and in truth. *"And whatsoever ye do in word or deed, do all in the name of the Lord Jesus..."* (Colossians 3:17).

Chapter Three

Determination in keeping in His Ways

"As newborn babes, desire the sincere milk of the word, that ye may grow thereby" (1 Peter 2:2), Apostle Paul giving guidance to the early Christians. Pure spiritual milk is the undiluted and unadulterated Word of God for growth in the Christian faith. In Romans 1:16 he refers to the gospel of Christ as **power of God** that brings salvation to everyone who believes. As a believer, in you is this power since you have been saved. God's Word will develop you, it will build you up (Acts 20:32). Be determined to know God's Word (The Bible). Study it for growth so you are not stunted in the faith. Nurse your faith to maturity. The Bibles records that the Berean Christians heard God's Word preached, and with great eagerness examined the Scriptures daily (Acts 17:11). In

2 Timothy 2:15, we are enjoined to study The Word so we can handle this message of truth correctly. By studying the Word, we receive wisdom and direction for life. The study and application of the Word in strict obedience keeps us on the right path. Practicing what the Word says keeps us secure. Jesus said to His followers in Luke 6:47-49 (NIV) *"As for everyone who comes to me and hears my words and puts them into practice, I will show you what they are like. [48] They are like a man building a house, who dug down deep and laid the foundation on rock. When a flood came, the torrent struck that house but could not shake it, because it was well built. [49] But the one who hears my words and does not put them into practice is like a man who built a house on the ground without a foundation. The moment the torrent struck that house, it collapsed and its destruction was complete."*

Putting our faith in God's Word is prerequisite for successful and fulfilling Christian life. Psalm 84:12 (NIV) *"Lord Almighty, blessed is the one who trusts in you"*. Abraham the father of faith pleased God because of his exceptional trust in God. The blessing and reward of his confidence in God transcended his generation *"...the promise comes by faith, so that it may be by grace and may be guaranteed to all Abraham's offspring... but also to those who have the faith of Abraham..."* (Romans 4:16 NIV), which includes the believers. The Bible in Galatians 3:29 states *"And if ye be Christ's, then are ye Abraham's seed, and heirs according to the promise."*

The Bibles tells us that *"...faith cometh by hearing, and hearing by the word of God"* (Romans 10:17). When we are consistently taught by the Word, the light of the glorious gospel shines in our hearts. Why not with Jesus? With all the privileges of brand new and everlasting life, benefit of becoming God's children and accompanying blessings. Being born of Him makes us one with Him. *"All honor to God, the God and Father of our Lord Jesus Christ; for it is his boundless mercy that has given us the privilege of being born again so that we are now members of God's own family. Now we live in the hope of eternal life because Christ rose again from the dead."*1 Peter 1:3 (TLB). Being God's children demand we live in conformity with Him. The Bible tells us in Ephesians 4:24 (NLT) to: *"Put on your new nature, created to* be like God—*truly righteous and holy.*" For these reasons, we must live conscious of God in us as well as conscious of who we are. Being God-conscious, we depend not on our physical senses but our the spiritual. Our love for God propels our actions. God's for us is beyond measure. In Ephesians 3:19 we read that His love for us goes far beyond knowledge; meaning it's so great it cannot be fully comprehended.

WHY NOT WITH JESUS? You too may want to ask those yet to know Him. God's Word in Hosea 10:12 (GNT) states "*...It is time for you to turn to me, your Lord, and I will come and pour out blessings upon you.*" We read of Cornelius in Acts 10:1-8 that he did not delay, and of the jailer in Acts 16:25-34, who also did not hesitate but took the opportunity to be saved.

To the one who is yet to receive Christ's salvation; God is good, He gives us His righteousness "*I am bringing my righteousness near, it is not far away; and my salvation will not be delayed...*" (Isaiah 46:13). This is only for those who will embrace this great offer. It is out of God's infinite mercy that He offers us His righteousness. Be wise and do not delay. This is God's gracious redemption package through Christ after the first man, Adam lost it in the Garden of Eden. This package offers man conformity with His Maker. *"It is true that through the sin of one man death began to rule because of that one man. But how **much greater is the result of what was done by the one man, Jesus Christ**! All who receive God's abundant grace and <u>are freely put right with him</u> **will rule in life through Christ**.[18] So then, as the one sin condemned all people, in the same way the one righteous act sets all people free and gives them life."* (Romans 5:17-18 GNT)

Christ's redemption work makes us come alive to God. The old ways gone and supplanted with a new and higher way that is dedicated to God. There is therefore now no record of wrong ever done because God sees and has a new you (Isaiah 43:25, John 1:29, Romans 4:7-8). Glory to God! He focuses on your present and future. By living this new and glorious life that is fully yielded and obedient to God, a future guaranteed in God awaits you (Jeremiah 29:11 GNT) because He will lead, guide and direct you.

"The righteous shall flourish like the palm tree: he shall grow like a cedar in Lebanon. 13 Those that be planted in the house of the Lord shall flourish in the courts of our God.
14 They shall still bring forth fruit in old age; they shall be fat and flourishing;
15 To show that the Lord is upright: he is my rock, and there is no unrighteousness in him" (Psalm 92:12-15).

Life with Jesus is life of glory and power. Proverbs 4:18 (NIV) tells us that *"The path of the righteous is like the morning sun, shining ever brighter till the full light of day."* God's light shine upon our ways to illuminate our path. This light shine by the help of the Holy Spirit, the Spirit of Truth that leads and guides the believer wherever he goes. The believer no longer walks in darkness or ignorance. The Holy Spirit even goes as far as showing the believer in Christ things that are yet to happen (John 16:13). Jesus will never leave nor forsake His own.

Stand strong in this new life that God has given you and in the righteousness purchased for you through the precious blood of Jesus.

"Seek good, not evil,
that you may live.
Then the Lord God Almighty will be
with you,
just as you say he is."
(Amos 5:14 NIV)

Chapter Four

Demonstrating the Life

"In the Lord's name, I tell you this. Do not continue living like those who do not believe. Their thoughts are worth nothing"
(Ephesians 4:17 NCV).

Now we live our lives totally submitted to the Master, Jesus our Example; walking in the light as He is in the light (1 John 1:5). As the attributes/light of the gospel shines through us, sin/darkness is dismissed

Having been made right with God and becoming the righteousness of God (2 Corinthians 5:21), our lives must make true reflections. As we live-out our new nature, the extra-ordinary life in us is activated.

As co-heirs with Christ (Romans 8:17), we no longer live the ordinary life, neither do we operate like the rest of the world (Romans 8:9) but like Jesus to whom we belong; Reason we are called Christians (Christ-like) -people who act like Christ. *"And be not conformed to this world: but be ye transformed by the renewing of your mind, that ye may prove what is that good, and acceptable, and perfect, will of God"* (Romans 12:2)

The moment we gave Jesus control and authority over our lives, we were translated into a system that is beyond this world. The life we now live must transcend the world's system; the reason our new life is called the transcendent life. We live above failure, defeat, sickness and poverty when we live by the Word. 1 John 4:9 *"In this was manifested the love of God toward us, because that God sent his only begotten Son into the world, that we might live through him."* The Bible describe life through Christ as incorruptible (1 Peter 1:23) and eternal (1 John 5:11-12).

With Jesus reigning in our lives, God's Spirit lives and abide with us (1 John 4:15, John 14:23). Zephaniah 3:17 states, *"The Lord thy God in the midst of thee is mighty; he will save, he will rejoice over thee with joy; he will rest in his love, he will joy over thee with singing."* We are God's delight. We reign with Him in this life. The Bible states in Romans 8:1 *"There is therefore now no condemnation to them which are in Christ Jesus, **who walk not after the flesh, but after the Spirit**."* This implies living the life of the Spirit of God; the old carnal ways (flesh) been replaced by the new (2 Corinthians 5:17). Life of the spirit prevails over the circumstances of this world, making us reign in life, as victors not victims (1 John 4:4). The new life demonstrates the nature and character of God.

"Now, therefore, you are no longer strangers and foreigners, but fellow citizens with the saints and members of the household of God" (Ephesians 2:19 NKJV) God is holy and lives in holiness hence we must live in conformity with His nature. God's Spirit (the Holy Spirit) who is our Guide (John 16:13) gives us direction for victorious living. He promises not to leave us as orphans but come to our aid. *"I will not leave you as orphans [comfortless, desolate, bereaved, forlorn, helpless]; I will come [back] to you"* (John 14:18 Amp). Life in God is Holy Spirit-assisted. For victorious

living, we must listen and obey when He speaks to our spirits.

This glorious living can reach the untold if those already saved make ourselves available in soul-saving action to bring others to the saving-power of our Lord Jesus Christ. We give others the opportunity of new life when we take the gospel to them. The Word of God tells us to make the gospel (the good news) of Christ available to others (Matthew 28:19-20). Romans 10:15 refers to it as **the gospel of peace**. By reaching out to others, we demonstrate of love Christ in us. Our message gives our hearers opportunity to respond to the love of God, get saved with eternal life (John 3:15).

God is not biased, He offered Jesus to die for all (John 3:16). Salvation comes to anyone who believe, who then become God's sons (1 John 3:1). Apostle Paul says to the Philippian Church *"May you **always be filled** with the fruit of your salvation—the **righteous character** produced in your life by Jesus Christ—**for this will bring much glory and praise to God**."* (Philippians 1:11 NLT). Our new nature produces and is demonstrated in fruits (lifestyle and attribute) of the Spirit (of God) such as love, joy, peace, patience, kindness, goodness, faithfulness, gentleness and self-control (Galatians 5:22-23 NLT). Due to this our new nature, we are no longer ruled by our flesh or senses but by God's Spirit. The Bible lets us know that those who live in the realm of the flesh cannot please God (Romans 8:8). They are not in sync with God and therefore cannot function at His level.

*"Now we have received, not the spirit of the world, but the **spirit which is of God**; that we might know the things that are freely given to us of God"* (1 Corinthians 2:12). His power, His nature and kind of life has all been given us! Salvation which took place in our spirit, regenerated us for divine access, divine insight, knowledge and understanding (Matthew 13:11) by which we know and discern the mind of God. This is joy of salvation. Apostle Paul relating the changes in himself, mentioned to King Agrippa the enablement and empowerment received due to his regeneration. He said to him in Acts 26:29 (NIV) *"I pray to God that not only you but all who are listening to me today may*

become what I am..." It takes a man who has experienced better life to speak like this.

Relationship with God enables for divine privileges. The Spirit of God in man makes him extra-ordinary. When God's Spirit came upon Saul, he prophesied (1 Samuel 10:9-11). He became anointed and extra-ordinary. This empowerment is hinged on God's Spirit and power upon the man Saul. For our well-being spiritually, the essential role of fellowship with God through prayers and study of His Word cannot be over-emphasised. Constant fellowship with God is of momentous benefits. Praying in the Holy Spirit (1 Corinthians 14:2 NLT) builds, deepens and strengthens our relationship with God.

Since prayer is two-way communication, it is important that our spirit is tuned to God in alertness so we can be sensitive to what God is saying and revealing to us in response. Jeremiah 33:3 (NIV) *"Call to Me, and I will answer you, and show you great and mighty things, which you do not know."*

"God is a Spirit: and they that worship him **must worship him in spirit and in truth"**

(John 4:24). Life in Christ is a life of the spirit and because God is a Spirit, it becomes the only way to fellowship with Him. *"...worship the Father in spirit and in truth. The Father is looking for those **who will worship him that way**"* (John 4:23 NLT). As we relate God in spirit and in truth, we develop intimacy with Him. To maintain this, Ephesians 6:18 tells us to pray in the Spirit. The homage of the heart is what is required rather than that of the lips. Praying/relating to God in the spirit **strengthens** the inner man (our spirit man), keeping us alert and alive to God. *"...that from his glorious, unlimited resources he will empower you with inner strength through his Spirit"* (Ephesians 3:16 NLT). The Amplified Bible puts it this way: *"... **to be strengthened** and **reinforced** with mighty power in the inner man by the [Holy] Spirit [**Himself indwelling your innermost being and personality**]."* With God's Spirit in man, victorious living is guaranteed.

Being born again or being born of God, what the Father requires is a sincere heart that is yielded to Him in the knowledge of His will. This is what demonstrates true sonship. *"When Jesus spoke again to the people, he* said, *"...I am the light of the world: he that followeth me shall not walk in darkness, but shall have the light of life."* (John 8:12). God's blessings flow in our lives when we abide in the light of God's Word through obedience. James 1:25 (NKJV) states *"...a doer of the work, this one will be blessed in what he does."* Disobedience severe our bond with God. We build solid foundation for the new life we possess when we are doers of God's Word (James 1:22). Obedience implies aligning with the will of God, it implies not compromising God's will but maintaining conformity regardless of circumstances or pressure. This is how we prove our love to the Father in return and this is how we stay committed to him. Loving the Father involves making sacrificial godly choices. Love for the Father compels us to obey Him. *"...Fear God, and keep his commandments: for this is the whole duty of man"* (Ecclesiastes 12:13).

The love, affection and the mercy that God showed us by the sacrifice of His Son, Jesus, redeemed us from darkness to light. This awesome privilege stepped us into the honourable position as joint heirs with Christ (Galatians 4:7). What a privilege we have in

Christ Jesus! He takes care of our need (1 John 5:14-15). When we face challenges, He enjoins us in Hebrews 4:16 to *"...come boldly unto the throne of grace, that we may obtain mercy, and find grace to help in time of need."* In God, we find all the help that we need. For He alone makes our ways perfect. When we are faced with challenges, we must hold-on to the Originator and the 'perfecter' of our faith (salvation). Hebrews 12:2 (NIV) states, *"fixing our eyes on Jesus, the pioneer and perfecter of faith. For the joy set before him he endured the cross, scorning its shame, and sat down at the right hand of the throne of God"*. We are the joy set before Him. We are His delight and hence should live as such. He scorned the shame of the cross for us and in the same manner, we too should scorn any reason to compromise His will. We now live for Christ. *"He died for everyone so that <u>those who receive his new life will no longer live for themselves. Instead, they will live for Christ</u>, who died and was raised for them"* (2 Corinthians 5:15 NLT). As we live this new life, holding on and anchoring on Jesus as our essence of life, we derive the entire pleasure of salvation package.

By our new nature we receive the gift of righteousness (Romans 5:17), the nature of God in true holiness. This is not just a position before God but a nature we must portray in relationship with others. The fruits of the Spirit of God in our new nature produces the following fruits (off-shoots/outcomes): **love**, **joy**, **peace**, **patience**, **kindness**, **goodness**, **faithfulness**, **gentleness** and **self-control** referred to as fruits of the Spirit (Galatians 5:22-23 NLT). The Bible tells us in John 15:4 to remain in Christ for us to continue to bear fruits.

It is our responsibility to keep and preserve the privilege of our adoption as God's children. With this consciousness, it is pertinent to remind ourselves to keep in line with the Father's will by obedience to His Words. Obedience to the Father secures glorious relationship with Him which amounts to wisdom for triumphant life. Living life being a **doer** of God's Word leads to numerous blessings. Jesus said to His disciples in the Book of John, chapter 15 that He is the true Vine. He tells us to remain in Him so we may bear fruit, that apart from Him we, struggle. John 15:4-16 (NIV) *"Remain in me, as I also* *remain in you. No branch can bear fruit by itself; it must <u>remain in the vine</u>. Neither can you bear fruit unless you remain in me.*

⁵ "<u>I am the vine</u>; you are the branches. If you remain in me and I in you, you will bear much fruit; <u>apart from me you can do nothing</u>. ⁶ If you do not remain in me, you are like a branch that is thrown away and withers; such branches are picked up, thrown into the fire and burned. ⁷ If you remain in me and my words remain in you, ask whatever you wish, and it will be done for you. ⁸ This is to my Father's glory, that you <u>bear much fruit, showing yourselves to be my disciples</u>.

*⁹ "As the Father has loved me, so have I loved you. Now remain in my love. ¹⁰ <u>If you keep my commands, you will remain in my love</u>, just as I have kept my Father's commands and remain in his love. ¹¹ I have told you this so that my joy may be in you and that your joy may be complete. ¹² My command is this: Love each other as I have loved you. ¹³ <u>Greater love has no one than this: to lay down one's life for one's friends</u>. ¹⁴ **You are my friends if you do what I command**. ¹⁵ I no longer call you servants, because a servant does not know* *his master's business. Instead, I have called you friends, for everything that I learned from my Father I have made known to you.* ¹⁶ *You did not choose me, but **I chose you and appointed you so that you might go and bear fruit—fruit that will last**—and so that whatever you ask in my name the Father will give you.*

Conclusion

In John 3:3, Jesus said, *"...Verily, verily, I say unto thee, except a man be born again, he cannot see the kingdom of God."* This means except a man has this new life (that only Jesus gives), he cannot experience the glory of God and eternity with Him. In the same vein, the fellowship and the communication of the Holy Spirit mentioned in 2 Corinthians 13:14 can only be experienced by those born of the Spirit. To be born of Him is to be able to partake of His special grace and power.

Apostle John remarked, *"Out of his fullness* **we have all received grace in place of grace** *already given"* (John 1:16 NIV). If anyone is in union with Christ, life for such a person, is from grace to grace, level to level and from glory to glory. It means that the fullness of the supply is constant and the power to receive increases with the use, or diminishes with the neglect. We must therefore put what we have received to work. Grace brings beauty and attraction. When you are full of God, you are automatically full of grace. We read of Elijah, Daniel and Apostle Paul who were full of God, hence full of grace and therefore lived extra-ordinary lives. These men were purpose-driven. They dominated situations that faced them, making notable impacts simply because they knew the true God. Christ conquered the world and gave us power to reign with Him. The life He has bought for us through His heavy sacrifice produces for us the higher life (life in its fullness). Jesus, in John 10:10 (NIV) states "... *I have come that they may have life, and have it to the full*". Jesus was purpose-driven. He stopped at nothing (Hebrews12:2) to give us the higher life. His purpose was to give us the actual life that God intends for man. Not life of oppression or helplessness but that of dominion, power and might. Life that is not subject to sin or the devil. Jesus came to give us the God kind of life (Zoë).

WHY NOT WITH JESUS?
For the Bible lets us know that
WHOEVER calls on His name
SHALL BE SAVED! (Acts 2:21)
What a grand privilege!

Jesus becomes Lord of your life the moment you pronounce Him so with your own mouth, recognising His sacrifice/death and resurrection (Romans 10:9). This ushers in the new life. By this message, we and our family can be saved (Acts 11:14). Jesus, being the true Light, anyone that 'walks' with Him will no longer walk in darkness. His wisdom makes you aware and knowledgeable to navigate your way through life. With Jesus, life becomes meaningful and purposeful (John 8:12). As you walk in Jesus, He will light-up your path (Proverbs 4:18).

Why walk in darkness and not with Jesus RIGHT-AWAY?

Life without Him is empty!

Have you made Him Lord of your life? Are you saved? Do you now have this new life? If your answer is yes, I say CONGRATULATIONS!!

The new life is invaluable, and reflects Christ. *"...he died for all, that they which live should not henceforth live unto themselves, but unto him which died for them, and rose again"* (2 Corinthians 5:15). Christ's ultimate sacrifice brought man back to God. Adam's sin severed us from God but Jesus' blood redeemed us to God. God so loved man that it cost Him the precious blood of His only son to reinstate man (John 3:16). God's love and mercy provided us the remission of sin. Hebrews 10:17 (NIV) states, *"Their sins and lawless acts, I will remember no more"*. Jeremiah 33:8 (NIV) *"I will cleanse them from all the sin they have committed against me and will forgive all their sins of rebellion against me"* says the Lord.

The redeemed man therefore must no longer sin because he has been bought with a price. He is now in God's image and his life must also depict God's love to others, and bring them also to the saving power of Christ. He lives a life of faith and commitment to God. Daniel was uncompromising and determined with his faith. He was focused to the point that his passion persuaded the king (Daniel 6:25-27).

"Then king Darius wrote unto all people, nations, and languages, that dwell in all the earth; Peace be multiplied unto you.
26 I make a decree, That in every dominion of my kingdom men tremble and fear before the God of Daniel: for he is the living God, and stedfast for ever, and his kingdom that which shall not be destroyed, and his dominion shall be even unto the end.
27 He delivereth and rescueth, and he worketh signs and wonders in heaven and in earth, who hath delivered Daniel from the power of the lions."

Daniel's attitude convinced the king. From notoriously felonious and aberrant life, Saul of Tarsus (Paul) became a great apostle of our Lord Jesus Christ. Quoting him in Galatians 2:20, *"I am crucified with Christ: nevertheless I live; yet not I, but Christ liveth in me: and the life which I now live in the flesh I live by the faith of the Son of God, who loved me, and gave himself for me."* These were the words of a new man in Christ. No longer in sin and death but in sync with Christ. *"For the wages of sin is death; but the gift of God is eternal life through Jesus Christ our Lord"* (Romans 6:23).

Ephesians 4:23-24 (NIV) enjoins us, *"to be made new in the attitude of your minds;* **24** *and to put on* **the new self, created to be like God in true righteousness and holiness**. Our new nature demand that we portray Christ in all our ways. This will mean giving Him first place in all that we do so we can operate in God's pre-ordained path-ways for our lives. Full submission to God is a demonstration of sonship and His Fatherhood over us. There is an assuring life in God. His plans are perfect and His ways are sure. Romans 8:32 *"He that spared not his own Son, but delivered him up for us all, how shall he not with him also freely give us all things?"*

Living The New Life

1. Love God and His Word
   (Deuteronomy 6:5, Luke 10:27)
2. Be committed in faith (Hebrews 6:1)
3. Be determined to obeying God's Word
   (Psalm 119:1-16)
4. Avoid distractions/retrogression
   (Psalm 85:8)
5. Avoid sin (Psalm 1:1-3)
6. Avoid past/old belief system
   (Galatians 5:1)
7. Study the Word of God/the Bible
   (2 Timothy 2:15, Joshua 1:8)

Salvation is a precious and special gift of God to all who believe (John 1:12). Salvation is an all-inclusive word of the gospel, gathering into itself all the redemptive acts and processes. It connotes deliverance, liberation, redemption, good health, provision, safety, victory, triumphant life and preservation. This is the salvation package that Christ's death and sacrifice brought us. His awesome act delivered us from slavery to safety (Romans 10:9-10), gave us power (Luke 10:19), healing to our bodies (Isaiah 53:3-5) and brought us forgiveness of sins (Colossians 1:12-14).

Event of Salvation:

- Belief of the Truth (Ephesian 1:13)
- Faith in the Blood (Romans 3:25)
- Confession (Romans 10:9, 1 John 1:9)
- True repentance (2 Corinthians 7:10 NCV)
- Sanctification of the Spirit (John 17:17)
- Grace through faith (Ephesians 2:8-9)
- Faith in His Name (Acts 4:12).

Through Christ:

- We have Liberty, because we now have the Spirit of freedom (Romans 8:15)
- We are No longer debtors to sin because the Spirit mortifies sin in us (Romans 8:12-13)
- His Intercession and that of the Holy Spirit which preserves us (Romans 8:26-27, 34).

Salvation Bundle:

- Redemption (Romans 3:24, 1 Corinthians 1:30
- New Creation (2 Corinthians 5:17)
- Nearness to God (Ephesians 2:13)
- Freedom from condemnation (Romans 8:1)
- Spirit of life (Romans 8:2)
- Love of God (Romans 8:39)
- Truth (John 8:32, John 17:17)
- Sanctification (John 15:3)
- Provision (2 Corinthians 9:8 Amp, Philippians 4:19)
- Wisdom (1 Corinthians 1:30)
- Health (1 Peter 2:24)
- Peace (Philippians 4:6-7)
- Abundance (2 Corinthians 8:9)
- Righteousness (2 Corinthians 5:21)
- Begetting (1 Corinthians 4:15)
- Hope (1 Corinthians 15:19)
- Joy (Romans 15:13)
- Liberty (Galatians 5:1)
- Establishment in God (2 Corinthians 1:21)
- Triumph/Victory (2 Corinthians 2:14, 1 Corinthians 15:57)
- All Spiritual Blessings (Ephesians 1:3, John 1:16 NCV)

- Power (1 Corinthians 4:20)
- Grace (2 Corinthians 12:9, John 1:17)
- Preservation (Jude 1:20-25)
- Eternal life (2 Timothy 1:10, John 3:16).

*"…just as Christ was raised from the dead through the glory of the Father, **we too may live a new life**."*
Romans 6:4 (NIV)

"He will also keep you firm to the end, so that you will be blameless on the day of our Lord Jesus Christ. ⁹ God is faithful, who has called you into fellowship with his Son, Jesus Christ our Lord."
1 Corinthians 1:8-9 (NIV)

Printed in the United States
By Bookmasters